Flutter into the Sunshine

Flutter into the Sunshine

ANISHA SURI

White Falcon
Publishing

www.whitefalconpublishing.com

Flutter into the Sunshine
Anisha Suri

www.whitefalconpublishing.com

Requests for permission should be addressed to
anishasuri1807@gmail.com

ISBN - 978-1-63640-707-4

Dedicated to the past you,
the present you, and the future you.

About The Author

 Anisha Suri was born and brought up in Delhi, India. She is currently in the United States, pursuing a PhD in Electrical and Computer Engineering from the University of Pittsburgh. She is an alumna of Apeejay School – Delhi, Indira Gandhi Institute of Technology – Delhi, and University of Southern California – Los Angeles. Her first poetry collection, *'Knots In My Soul Thread'* was published in 2018. She runs a personal blog on Instagram and Facebook called The Poetic Instincts. For fun, she likes to bike and explore coffee shops. Her reading interests include non-fiction books on inspiration and self-transformation, historical fictions, Hindu mythology, and fictional murder mysteries. A researcher by profession and a poet at heart, Anisha believes that ideas and words can change the world.

 anishasuri1807@gmail.com

 @thepoeticinstincts

About The Book

Flutter into the Sunshine is a collection of thirty poems spread into five sections: *Life and Musings, A Feeling Called Love, Breaking Free and Marching On, Good Vibes, and Self-Love Above All.* In this collection, the author plays with elements of nature – the sky, the ocean, and the seasons, among others, and blends them with colours and moods. Time remains a subject that the author brings up often. The power of Yellow is highlighted, as also suggested by *Sunshine* in the title. The poems talk of being a light in the dark, refusing to lose hope, believing in the power of love, and marching ahead despite the obstacles. *Flutter* your way out. Be like a butterfly that acknowledges its limits but also keeps exploring invisible lands of flowers.

Meet The Team

This book is made possible by synergetic team efforts. Let me introduce you to the talented women I had the pleasure and honor of working with.

Illustrators

Aastha is an architect and loves traveling, reading, and trying all kinds of crafts. A big F.R.I.E.N.D.S. buff and animal lover!

Rivina is a Business Analyst by profession. Doodling and baking are her therapy techniques. She loves traveling, dogs, beaches, and throwing parties!

Tanvi is an architect and entrepreneur by profession, and an artist by passion. She loves to read and doodle while talking on the phone.

Editors

Aditi is a banker by profession and a procrastinator who loves to rhyme. She enjoys reading books and is always ready to dance to Bollywood songs.

Anaies is an engineer by education, data scientist by profession and a passionate individual who loves traveling, reading, and spending time with nature.

Divyasha is a Strategy Consultant by profession. She lives in Munich. Her latest book, *Tch Tch Tch*, a collection of contemporary short stories, was released in 2021.

Ruchismita is a Business Analyst at TCS and loves to travel, write and binge watch Korean dramas in her free time.

Preface

Most individuals pick up reading as a hobby when they are growing up, likely during middle - high school. I was never into reading back then. I would rather solve an extra mathematics problem or play another game of ping-pong than read a novel. As they say, I probably never found the right book. During my undergraduate studies, I realized what I had missed out on. It was Dan Brown and John Green's works that made me fall in love with reading books. As for poetry, I used to write poems in my mother tongue, Hindi, as well as in English. I find poems short, sweet, and impactful in only a few words. I write to connect with a reader who is on the path of self-discovery; who is navigating challenges with a courageous smile; who spreads love, values freedom, and is trying to inculcate within themselves the virtue of gratitude. My writings deal with the philosophy of being content with what one has, having patience, and always working towards becoming a better version of the unique self we are.

Balancing career commitments as a researcher and a hobbyist writer has been interesting so far. Both require creative writing skills; one is scientific while the other is more of an art. I enjoy my research work, and I feel energized after writing a poem. Pursuing a hobby doesn't feel burdensome to me; it feels like an investment in myself, and more of a self-care strategy. I think more millennials, and following generations, are trying to experiment with their interests, and trying to find their "Ikigai," the Japanese philosophy of life. Sometimes one becomes too attached to consequences and outcomes, which creates fear and an inability to try. If we start something new, we should focus on our actions and intentions, letting time take its course. An improvement in skills is felt with practice, giving us the confidence to keep going.

My first collection of poems, *Knots In My Soul Thread* was published in 2018. At the time, I already knew that a second collection would happen, but didn't know when. That's the deal with creative writing; I feel you cannot force it out of you, the process is gradual. Here, I present to you my second collection of poems, *Flutter into the Sunshine*. In this collection, I play with elements of nature, blend them with colors, and urge individuals to both stand out, as well as blend into the community. Time remains a subject that I bring up now and then. I highlight the power of Yellow, of being the light in dark, refusing to lose hope, believing in love, and marching ahead despite obstacles. Through these writings, I urge you to realize the infinite you, and to acknowledge the purity reflected in the eyes of the people you meet. I truly hope that teenagers, young adults, and grown-ups will all relate to some of the ideas I present through these writings. I hope you feel the emotions and moods behind these writings. May these poems make you ponder, make you believe, and make you smile.

Happy reading!

Anisha Suri

Acknowledgements

I want to thank the invisible, infinite force that lies within us. This force creates possibilities beyond the imagination of the human mind. Persistence, Patience, and Passion are the qualities I would like to acknowledge – these played a key role in materializing *Flutter into the Sunshine*.

I want to express my sincere gratitude towards the dynamic and creative female friends who have helped in editing the poems - Anaies, Aditi, Divyasha, and Ruchismita; and in creating the amazing sketch work - Aastha, Rivina, Tanvi. I connected with all of them during different phases of life. Aastha and Tanvi are my friends from Apeejay School, Delhi, where I pursued my high school education. I met with Aditi, Divyasha, Rivina, and Ruchismita during my undergraduate engineering studies at Indira Gandhi Institute of Technology, Delhi. Divyasha is a published writer herself and has been an inspiration to me. I bonded with Anaies during my postgraduate studies at the University of Southern California.

The academic institutions I have been a part of have played a major role in shaping my scientific interests, as well as giving me the bandwidth to experiment with literary writings. I am grateful for the writing opportunities and participation in intra and inter-school activities that teachers at Apeejay encouraged me to pursue. My current mentors and advisors at University of Pittsburgh know about my poetry interests and keep telling me to bring that creativity in scientific writing as well.

I also want to thank Dr. Rajiv Ranjan Dwivedi, Associate Professor of English at Delhi Technological University; Shivani Verma, English teacher at Apeejay School, Delhi; and my mom, Anita Suri for reviewing the initial draft of the manuscript. Their feedback helped me improve the writing and expression.

Thanks to my mom, my dad, Prof. Pradeep Kumar Suri, my brother, Tushar Suri, and my partner, Puneet for their constant cheering. My family and friends have always supported my creative endeavours. I owe all my achievements to the wonderful encouragement they provide. The unfiltered feedback from them keeps me going - they are the first buyers of my work, first critics, and my first fans.

Finally, thank you to all the readers who have read my work, and to those who have picked up my poems for the first time. Thank you for believing in a young writer.

Anisha Suri

Life and Musings

☀ Knots in My Soul Thread

☀ Building Walls

☀ Silent Observer

☀ Haywire

☀ Be Both

☀ Then, Now, and Later

☀ You Are Your Thoughts

Flutter into the Sunshine

Knots in My Soul Thread

Entangled.
Trying to sort, before, still, forever.
There are knots,
knots in my soul-
like thread:
Visible stitches,
Visible patches,
Not visible to the naked eye,
but to the naked soul.

Inseparable, they never end -
the thread and its knots.
The lessons, the promises.
The hopes, the magic.
.

.

Knots in my soul thread.

Flutter into the Sunshine

Building Walls

I walk into a bookstore
and see the walls
reflecting my life -
the packed shelves: my past
the partially filled ones: my present
and the empty ones: my future.
My stories, they hold
told and untold.
And all those who know me -
can they ever really know me?

Ah, maybe not.
Everyone is busy
unintentionally.
Seeing their reflections
building similar walls
in that very bookstore.
Can I ever really know anyone?

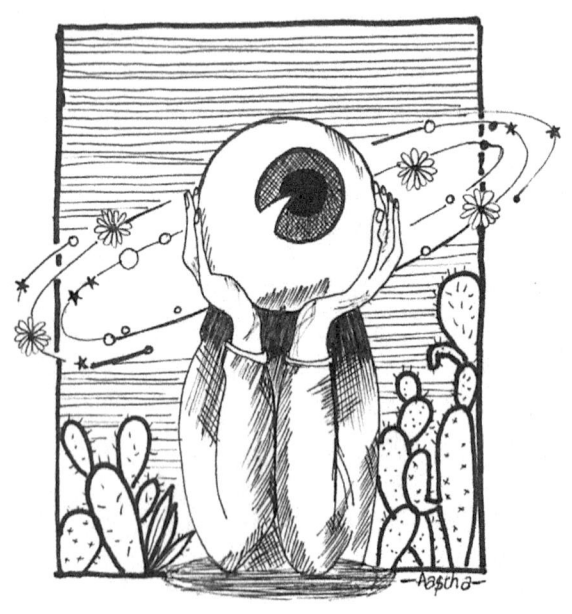

Flutter into the Sunshine

Silent Observer

Standing still
and watching
the world –
A swarm of people
pacing in Brownian motion.

You could be different and special and unique –
and you'll probably still
go unnoticed.
Who knows my story –
you ask yourself.
Does anyone care?

You are not doing this for them – you remind yourself.
You are not doing this for them!
Maybe you have a family to feed
or maybe you are meant to be
alone
navigating the world
trying to fit in.
Who knows?

Standing still
but acutely conscious
of the world
of the people.
Silent, but with a voice
with choices, dreams, hopes
all hidden in their story
if only someone cares
to listen.

Flutter into the Sunshine

Haywire

I dream
of falling teeth.
I struggle to pick them up
and put them back in place
one by one -
but they keep slipping from my fingers
and flying back
to my old self.
My eyes
struggle to open,
to wake up and stop,
stop the chaos,
to hold the teeth in place but,
they fly away still.
I sense,
They fear change -
Change in time,
in place, in people.
Crumbling teeth, crumbling self,
I lose control of my mind,
of me.

But my heart beats warmth
and love and hope.
It stands by me.
I am surprised it can still *believe*.
It keeps me sane.
It wins every time
in this battle within me
that I can't stop fighting.

Flutter into the Sunshine

Be Both

Blue or red?
I thought
I was both.

I became
the red sun.
Bold and Mystical
Why not a yellow one?
But yellow is too mainstream!

My aura,
I chose to paint blue –
Like the sky
But isn't that mainstream?
You ask.
Sure, it is!
Familiar and comfortable.

.

.

Be both.

Flutter into the Sunshine

Then, Now, and Later

To begin, a child
Says her first 'Hello'
Yellow and vibrant
Caressed and pampered
Sensitive skin and sensitive mind
Dolls, toys, and a promised fairyland.

Then, a teen
Reluctant and unsteady,
Conscious of her body,
Gradually accepting of her imperfections.
Then, glowing skin and glowing youth
Dreams, hopes and a promised world.

A young woman now,
Mother, Daughter, Wife, and such labels
Pride and independence.
Skin scarred with sacrifice.
Yet - hopeful and strong.
Gentle, kind and a promised life.

Later, a woman,
Who barely walks or talks.
Dark and dull like rotten ash
Wrinkled skin and wrinkled memories.
Lost, forgotten, and still waiting
for her promised meal.

Flutter into the Sunshine

You Are Your Thoughts

Like the sea of clouds
hanging in the sky,
I sometimes see my thoughts
Clustered
Dense and vivid.
With patterns
Just like clouds.
And just like clouds
some bring storm and rain,
some keep away the heat, the light,
and some, with a purpose unknown,
growing unsupervised.

Mostly untamed, uncontrollable,
They deserve, for once,
a peaceful corner in a cluttered sky.

People say: 20s are crazy,
I insist it is not the age.
It is the time, the place, the people -
somehow becoming a part of you.
And after all,
you are not your body.
You are your thoughts.

A Feeling Called Love

☀ Her Arms

☀ Can a Butterfly Stay?

☀ My Idea of Love

☀ I Wrote in Red Ink

☀ I Am Blessed to Have You

☀ Your Eyes

Flutter into the Sunshine

Her Arms

Open arms, moist eyes,
she was trying to cover
it all with
her pretty dress.
Her hands,
running on my face,
fingertips
trying to feel a change.
'Blood and Bones don't change'
my eyes tell her.
Water had reached the edge
but,
neither
let a drop fall.
Time made us strong,
I could tell.
I hugged her tightly.
The safest place on Earth,
her arms.
I am home.

Flutter into the Sunshine

Can a Butterfly Stay?

You make me unwind.
I was like a butterfly,
fluttering to fly,
to match the birds.
But I can't reach that high.
Dejected, I sit and stare,
at the clouds that I can't touch,
I give up.
Just then,

I see a hand offered to me.
Thrilled, I grab it with hope,
I take a chance.
It was you!
You lift me up,
you make it so easy.
I go beyond the sky
waving at the stars.
I feel so high
and so now I follow you.
You are like a flower to me,
a flower that I'll never want to lose.
I want just this one flower,
I will water it,
make it immortal.
To stay on one flower,
I used to think,
was not my nature.
I now think,
one can indeed make a butterfly stay,
love and patience are all it takes.

Flutter into the Sunshine

My Idea of Love

You wear your soul
beneath your skin.
But to rip your skin,
watch your blood drip,
drops struggling to find
a place to rest,
gravity in charge,
the ground flooded.
There isn't any room to contain it.

To make such efforts
Just to know you?
Layers beneath layers
still failing to see through you,
I am no more up for it!
Skin deceives, every time.
If not today,
you will realize that soon.
That's why
I carry my soul
in my eyes.

The effortlessness –
I love the idea of
naked eyes.
I would rather
you see my tears
than have you rip my skin.
That's my idea of love.

Flutter into the Sunshine

I Wrote In Red Ink

I wrote in red ink
a letter to my start,
a letter to my end.

When I feel lost,
you remind me
of my being,
of my good deeds,
of my talents,
of my innocence,
you make me happy.

Why would I not choose you?
I will, always.
You fear I will
find someone better.
Better than you?
There's none!

When I just
cry out my thoughts
you catch all my tears
and turn them into diamonds
With such ease

Why will I not choose you?
My ink may fade away
but my letter will reach you
before that, I assure you.

Flutter into the Sunshine

I Am Blessed to Have You

When the sky falls off
and the galaxy is naked,
When the angels disappear
and the moon is gone,
When the Earth is out of light
and nature is playing games,

My friend,
I will remind you
of what you are truly capable of.
You will shine so bright,
the Earth will be flabbergasted,
Angels will return and the sky will lift back up,
In your ears, they'll all mutter,
'I am blessed to have you.'

Flutter into the Sunshine

Your Eyes

Your raw eyes
tell a story,
looking for magic,
within a wonderland.
Your hair,
swaying with the wind,
I can see them
wanting to escape.
I like how they are messy,
just like both of our lives.
That smile,
almost a smirk,
hinting that you don't care,
but you do.
I see it –
in your eyes.

Breaking free and marching on

Flutter into the Sunshine

If Only Love Could Save Me

If only love could save me,
I would be floating,
but here I am
on the ocean bed,
tied in chains,
trying to pull myself up.
I hope to swim one day.
I was told
that I was loved,
when I should have been told
that I was brave,
brave enough
to break the chains
and rise up,
brave enough
to learn to swim
even in chains.

Flutter into the Sunshine

The Rusted Cage

Empty cage!
Who let her out?
Well-fed
secure and pampered.
How will
she survive now?

Locked wings.
A predictable life.
She was caged.

'In discomfort alone, she found comfort.'

She let herself out
into uncertainty.
And now she *lives*,
not just survives.

The rusted cage–
rusted by her tears
never craves
her return.

Flutter into the Sunshine

Slow, but Go

I too have seen the Sun
but black and not yellow,
I am told,
'but the sky is so clear
and the sun couldn't be more yellow'
and well,
It has always been like that!

It is uncommon
and clearly unclear.
Maybe what's happening right now is,
the clouds are hiding the Sun
and making it black!

My life, I see
is seeking
that one star
that one energy
that is enough to inspire.

Uneasy right now,
on the way to gaining clarity,
my motto remains
'Slow, but go.'

Keeping my calm,
taking my time
because I know
once found,
that one purpose
will complete my life.

Flutter into the Sunshine

Taking Chances

Ever thought
Of the chances you take
To rebuild yourself
To become new
From the same old you?

Trying to play it safe.
But once again it's time,
to make that choice!

If you don't risk it,
you will never know!
So, set your anchor and sail
Go forth and fail!

All will be worth
the taste of the rainstorm.
Even the sight of your wrecked ship
Will amuse you, you'll see!
And you'll never fear
Starting it all over, again.
And again.

Flutter into the Sunshine

Reimagine

It is taking time
to learn
the ways of the world.
The real world
is not what I imagined
or rather,
was made to imagine.

I see myself trapped
in a school uniform -
outperforming and acing,
how less I cared
about the world.

I feel stuck in the puddle,
wanting to be a stream,
if not an ocean.

I feel stuck in the yellow,
wanting to be a Rubik's cube,
if not a rainbow.

I have decided
to allow
myself some time,
to reimagine.
This time
with the realism
that the world has taught.

Flutter into the Sunshine

Look Back

Look back
Look back often
See how far you have come
There was a time
You feared climbing
You feared falling

Feel proud
Of overcoming it all
Of taking that first step
Look back
Look back often
See how far you have come

Good Vibes

Flutter into the Sunshine

Free Spirit or a
Controlled Flame

'Free spirit, yet a
controlled flame' –
that's who I want to be!
To light that one flawlessly shaped flame,
countless matchsticks had to die.
No, I won't burn out soon, I promise!
Contained and controlled.
Watchers, share my light!
And, let me borrow yours.
'Humanity triumphs'
for they did no sin.
You owe it to them,
the ones who burnt out black,
just to make sure you stayed yellow.
Keep this fire burning!
For many are yet
finding their way!
To *their* yellow
and beyond.

Flutter into the Sunshine

Tell Me Your Yellows

I don't want to know your grays,
I have my own to handle.
Tell me your yellows,
your rainbows,
your ideas
to change the world.
Yes, tell me all of it!
Listening to your grays
or recounting to you mine
is exhausting our energy and time.
So the next time we talk
why not choose the bright side
and leave the dark aside.

Shades of You

I have seen you
Beat the cold without
The cover of leaves
And I have seen
You gift the birds
With a nest made of leaves

I have seen you stand bare,
Unnoticed,
On the verge of giving up.
I have seen you
Lit with all the colors of the rainbow,
Beautiful without ego

I have seen you grow
I have seen you fall
Seen how you remain the same
Changing yet unchanged.

I have seen you in your good times
And seen you in your bad times.
In all the seasons
You stand tall,
Undeterred and grounded
Isn't it amazing?
You inspire me
Without saying a word.

Flutter into the Sunshine

I Am the Cosmos

Cutting sharp
through the clouds,
I will find a way home.
I am not a spacecraft
in want of reaching the stars,
for I am the cosmos myself!

I have come this far
and I will travel farther
I'll walk through my fears
over beds of broken glass
I'll untangle my waves
that are stuck in the ocean grass

I will strive hard to know -
the vastness of the skies
the expanse of the lands and
the depths of the waters

I promise to live my life
harmonising with nature -
Skies, lands, oceans, and all.

Flutter into the Sunshine

Roots

And when I feel lost,
I go back
to my roots.
Unvalued then,
they are all that I have now.
Bearing weight
since the onset of it all,
do you see them complain?
Holding the tree together,
Against odd winds and floods,
roots don't fear.
Hold on to them!
Tight and near.
For, leaves will blow,
flowers will fall,
but roots will stay,
singing your glory,
reminding you of yourself
even when you fail.

Self-Love Above All

☀ The Love You Seek

☀ Alone, but With Yourself

☀ The Light Within

☀ Painting a Better Version

☀ My Shades

☀ A Self-Portrait

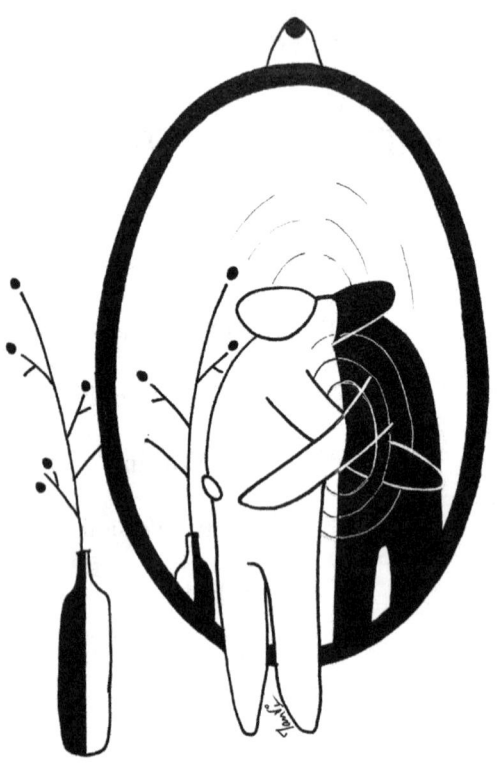

Flutter into the Sunshine

The Love You Seek

Warm and red,
scared and lonely eyes
looking for acceptance,
looking for love.
Love found.

The highs, the lows
cold and blue,
scared and lonely eyes
looking for a room,
a room to hide,
to avoid love.
Looked up.
A room found.

In the room -
looked around
found a mirror!
I realized who I needed.

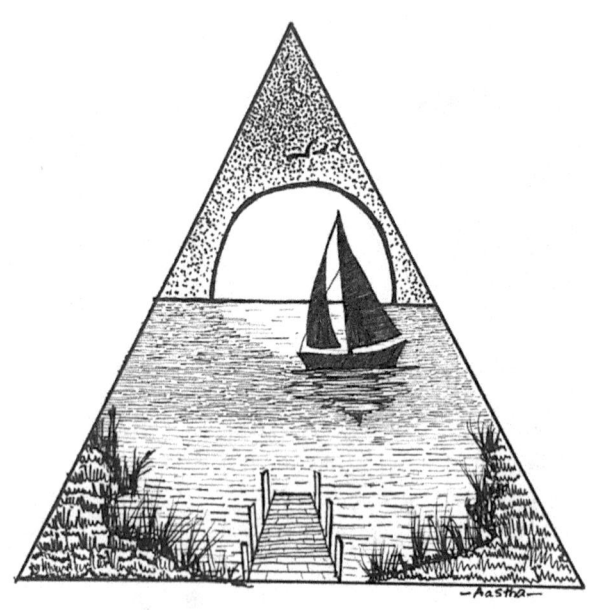

Flutter into the Sunshine

Alone, but With Yourself

No friend to console
No teacher to guide.
You are alone, left to fight.

No school to go.
No one to support.
You are alone in your own boat.

No praise, no charm.
No one who understands.
You are alone, in your nightmare.

No tears, no laughter.
No rules to follow.
You are alone, life seems to be hollow.

No work, no talks.
No concentration or coordination.
You are alone, with the feeling of alienation.

No emotions, no feelings.
No one seems to be near or dear.
You are alone, fighting your fear.

No curiosity, no pleasure.
No agility, just dullness.
You are alone, only silence and emptiness.

No one, nobody.
Nowhere, nothing.
You are alone, you cannot think.

But how can you always be alone,

When you are always with yourself.
It is not the time to run, hide or escape
but, time to give yourself some time,
to realize your real self,
and look for hope.

Rise and get back to life.
Appreciate the light in you.
Listen, it's not only about you.
Connect the dots!
Move to a new boat.
Set the anchor right.
Row again with an even greater force!
Remember,

You might be alone,
But always with yourself.

Flutter into the Sunshine

The Light Within

I slammed the door,
shut the window,
in one corner
of the four cornered room,
I sit vulnerable and scared.
no sunshine I want
it is too bright for me -
the world
advancing
at the speed of light.

Just when
I was becoming unsure
of my abilities,

Stars in my head
shone so bright.
Darkness was overruled,
giving me courage
to add my light
to the bright world
and make it brighter.
Depriving the world
of the unique light you have
is never a good idea.

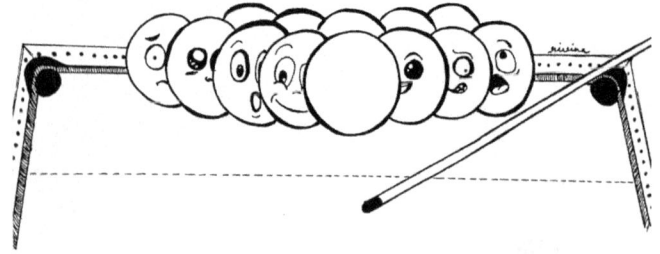

Flutter into the Sunshine

Painting a Better Version

Dancing on the snooker table
in the game of numbers,
I try to fit in everyday
in every sphere
of life.
Striped or Solid?
Nope,
I don't come labelled.
I change colors.
I cherish my yellow but
I don't forget my blues.
I keep them all,
painting a better version
of myself, everyday

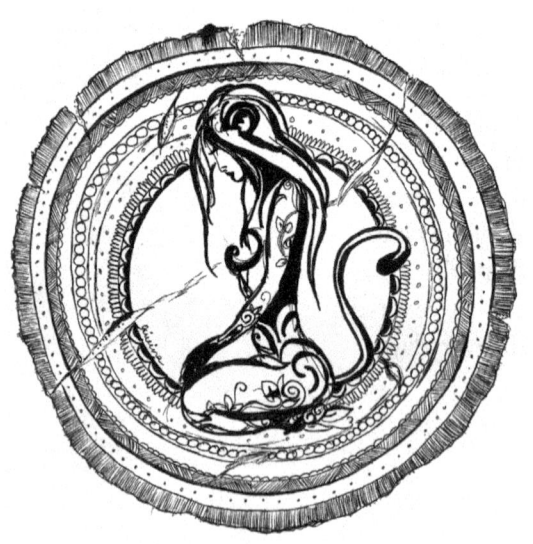

Flutter into the Sunshine

My Shades

Half asleep, half awake
I lay down to regain my strength
The naive keep wondering
'I gave up'
Really?
I am a symbol of valour
But I do have my shades
Attacking is one
Soaking the sun and
Regaining my energy
Another.
Watch what you think, fella.

Flutter into the Sunshine

A Self-Portrait

A pink silhouette
Of incomplete dreams
Of infinite desires
Of intuitive temperament
Of insignificant
yet significant changes

Of being one of a kind
A poem irreplaceable
Of being written by who?
Nature, time and most of all - YOU
Of believing in you
And of loving what you do

Of being the snow
And holding on to the leaves
Of refusing to melt into the falling dew
and of you committing to yourself.

CPSIA information can be obtained
at www.ICGtesting.com
Printed in the USA
BVHW032129251122
652777BV00016B/1084